Fat Jack Had a Heart Attack And Now He's Cookin' Lean!

How to cook low fat, low salt and actually
have your wife and kids eat the food.

Losing weight without speed so's you can regain or maintain
your health, self-respect and a fine sense of humor.

By

Fat Jack
(A.K.A. John P. White)

**Fat Jack Had a Heart Attack
And Now He's Cookin' Lean!**

Copyright Year: 2007
Copyright Notice: by John P. White.

All rights reserved.

The above information forms this copyright notice:

© 2007 by John P. White.

ISBN 978-0-6151-8971-0

Contents

Introduction

About This Book

About Cookin' Lean

Exercise

Salads

Soups, Stews and Stewps

Entrees, Sides, and everything else that isn't soup, salad or dessert

Desserts

Conlcusion

About the Author

Contact Information

Introduction

Fat Jack had a Heart Attack
And now he's cookin' lean!

February of 2006 I was researching new recipes south of Alamosa, well actually, I was at my son's basketball game. Anyway, I was feeling sort of odd—I had a really sore neck and the skin in that area felt kinda like your foot does when it goes to sleep. I had been feeling that off and on for a couple days. That night I didn't feel well laying down, and had trouble getting to sleep. The next morning I was nauseous still had a pain in the neck and felt like I'd swallowed a golf ball that was stuck in my chest. I decided to go to the hospital where I was informed I was having a heart attack. After a couple stents the docs informed me that while I wasn't going to die right off, I had to change my lifestyle. Since the whole emergency room-hospital thing wasn't near as much fun as it looks on TV, and since I can't really afford any more of those delicate little medical bills, I decided that maybe they were right.

I gotta tell you. I really had a good time writing recipes that were high fat and high salt. I really had a good time eating all that stuff. But they're telling me now that it was killing me. And if you made much of my stuff, or if you eat like I did, it's killing you too. Sorry, I really didn't know or believe it anyway. But now I do, so there's going to be some changes made in my cooking. *I refuse to eat tasteless crap and so should you!* So everything you read here will actually have flavor. Bear in mind, though, salt can be replaced only with salt. So you just have to get used to it. Took me, the wife and the kids about a month. Also remember that besides heredity and smoking, stress is *the* top cause for heart disease, so if you're going to totally stress out over your diet and how much salt you're eating, you might be hurting yourself more than helping. Moderation is the key, as someone famous once said. Anyway go walk around the block, 'cause you know you need the exercise, then go home and make something from the following pages.

Love and kisses,
John

About This Book

Now you can live the steady conservative life and just use this book as another cookbook to lose on the shelf. You can do that. But what I really want you to do is embrace your inner savage and take, cut, tear, rip or otherwise remove the pages of the book as you you use them. Try to not tear up the writing too much, we're gonna need that later. Then take the one you use, then put it in a sheet proctector like you get at the office supplies store and put that in a loose leaf notebook that you got when you picked up the sheet protectors. There is madness to my method and I'm offering you a rare chance to run naked through the woods with me on it.

Here's the theory, which I might add has worked pretty well for me in the past: Each page is in a sheet protector inside the notebook, or it will be when you stick 'em all in the protectors. This way, you can choose which recipes you want to use for say the next five nights. Pull them out and take them to the store with you so you have a list of ingredients to buy. Put them back when you get home, and open to the proper page when you cook. The sheet protectors uh, protect (no, duh) the recipes so you don't coat them in spilled food and whatnot and they won't get lost, shredded or destroyed like those little 3" x 5" cards. Put the recipes only on the front-facing sides of the protectors which allows you to add your own recipes on the back side. That last bit explains why each page is printed on only one side, see? You can also use glue sticks to stick recipes cut from magazines and newspapers or those 3" x 5" cards you have scattered all over the kitchen to the back of one and add those. Or you can use the backsides to add notes, changes or magic spells to enchance the recipe or turn Aunt Martha into a newt.

If you can't bring yourself to cut out the pages, then that glue stick will still allow you to make this book into your main reciepe book by sticking stuff on the blank pages. Clever, eh? But that's why I make the big bucks . . . So, go nuts and find something to cook. Why are you standing there? Turn the page, willya?

About Cookin' Lean

When they told me I had to change my ways (yikes!) I thought it was going to be really hard to go low fat. I thought the low salt would be easy. Wrong. I had it just backwards. You see, while I always thought all the flavor was in the fat, it just ain't so. Most of the stuff I cooked that cut out the fat the wife and kids didn't even notice. The salt. My God, the salt. It's in everything, tons of it. And we've gotten way dependent on it. The first dish I cooked with no salt was awful. It was the first dish Eiko the German Kid (our foreign exchange student) refused to eat in six months of living with us. Even Boomer the Cow Dog hesitated before he ate it. I suspect Boomer only ate it so as to not set any dangerous precedents about turning down food. Hell, I didn't even like it. It's not in this book. But you can overcome a lack of salt and still have the food taste good.

Anyway, this section is about what to do differently, what to substitute for what and a few brand names for stuff that tastes good and isn't loaded with salt, fat or both.

First off, read labels. You'll be astounded at what they're foisting off on us as food, not to mention the insane amount of sodium in packaged foods.

Substitutions:
- For cream use condensed skim milk, sometimes called skim evaporated milk—I haven't tried but I'm told it will even whip.
- For cream also try no fat plain yogurt mixed with some no fat sour cream.
- They now have fat-free heavy cream in the markets, though damned if I know how they do that!
- For soy sauce use Braggs Liquid Aminos, I know, odd name but less than ¼ the sodium.
- For lard use olive or canola oil.
- For butter use Smart Balance There's some other brands but they don't taste as good.
- For mayonaise—ummm, mayo—mix 2/3 mayo with 1/3 non-fat yogurt, same taste 1/3 less fat.
- For ice cream use sherbet.
- For eggs use eggbeaters--the kids made me father's day breakfast with 'em, lied and told me they were real eggs. I believed 'em and they were pretty ok. Kinda hard to do over-easy though. Great for cooking with and work just like real eggs in that situation.
- Use the various low or no salt versions of stuff like tomato sauce, ketchup and so forth, but keep some of the regular around—you can mix them and reduce the salt content to a reasonable level. Other stuff like this is chicken broth and various soups.
- Mix in some Worcestershire sauce, a bunch of no salt tomato sauce, ketchup and a little A-1 into your favorite barbecue sauce to reduce the salt content.
- Find no salt seasonings like taco and fajita at the health food store, usually in the bulk spices section.

Sly Tricks:
- Use no salt in cooking at all, save that in the processed foods you absolutely have to use. Make up for it by increasing the other flavors—spice much more heavily, learn to love lots of garlic, make friends with balsamic vinegar. Garlic and vinegar are keys to low salt cooking, experiment with them. Let those who are weak add salt at the table, but rag on them mercilessly when they do. Be advised it will take a couple weeks to get used to the new taste.

- Swear off frying and grill everything. If you fry it all the fat stays in the pan and lots of times you have to add fat to keep stuff from sticking. If you grill most of the fat in the food hits the fire, which incidentally makes it taste better. If you must fry, use just a couple teaspoons of oil, when it's cooking good and/or starting to stick, add some no-fat, low sodium chicken broth.

- If you're going to make taco meat, sloppy joes or any other busted up hamburger dish, grill the hamburger well done first, then let it cool a bit. Then take it in and break it up in a skillet. You'll be amazed at how little fat there is in it. To get the seasonings to take, add a little chicken stock to replace the fat.

- Slice potatoes like french fries, scatter on a Pam sprayed baking sheet, spray some Pam on the 'taters and bake for 30-40 minutes at 450. Amazingly good, especially if you use sweeter potatoes like white rose, reds or Yukon gold.

- Get some spray bottles for olive oil and canola oil. Just a small spritz will often times be enough to sauté stuff. Lots cheaper than Pam too and lacks the stuff that screws up non-stick surfaces. Also use the chicken broth trick mentioned earlier.

- To make roux, put two tablespoons olive oil in the pan and half a cup of chicken stock with a like amount of flour. Cook as usual, works great for thickening. Same trick works for sautéing mushrooms, onions, crab, lobster (Mmmm. Lobster.) or what have you.

- For pork and white fish, season heavily with dill weed. Sounds odd I know, but works really well and it's strong enough you won't miss the salt. Cook both on the grill.

- For burgers, meatballs, sloppy joes or what have you, mix ground beef with ground turkey or chicken—more beef if that's the primary flavor you're looking for although the kids like a 50-50% mix if it's seasoned up well. Add some plain instant oatmeal to stretch it some.

- Mrs. Dash and the like—sold as a salt substitute, it's not. Salt is the only substitute for salt. They are, however, really good spice mixes that may make you forget you wanted the salt. Maybe. Or not.

- Less. If you can't abide the low salt/fat version of something, use the regular version but use less. Maybe even just a little. Example: Low fat cheese tastes like wax, won't melt and is generally yucky. So, just use the regular stuff but not much, say one tablespoon on a taco instead of two pounds like you used to do, get it? Another good trick—mix 2/3 real mayonaise with 1/3 non-fat yogurt, it's a little soupy but retains the taste for 1/3 less salt and fat.

Good Brands to try:
- Naked Juice Blue Machine—tasty and one bottle contains no salt, no fat and 16 grams of fiber, mostly the really good soluble variety. Also contains blueberries and others with all sorts of good junk in 'em. I try to drink two a day.

- 505 salsa—just the red, the green has more salt. Red's about 120-mg sodium per 2 tbls bad.

- Santa Fe Salsa—about 102 mg salt per two tbls.

- Braggs Liquid Aminos—unappealing name for a really good soy sauce substitute, less than ¼ the sodium in *Light* soy sauce.

- Check out the local health food store, many have lots of low fat stuff and sometimes low salt. By the same token, beware of organic and health food labeled foods as many are really good on fat but ignore the salt issue.

- No Yolks noodles—taste just like regular egg noodles without the cholesterol and fat.

- Kashi breakfast cereal—tasty, high fiber, low fat, high protein, what's not to like?

Labels! Read them. Make it your new hobby. Make note of the good stuff and the bad stuff alike.

Exercise

I'm possibly the laziest person in the world, except for my kids of course. Furthermore, I have some truly poorly operating knees. Thus I was getting about zero exercise before the big event. I used to ski, rock climb, hike, backpack, hunt, fish, golf, and other stuff like that. Since the knees started to go I gradually gave it all up. With the kind attentions of the Mercy Hospital Wellness Center rehab program, I'm back to where I can actually walk a couple miles without requiring a stick or the kids to carry me back to the truck. I can walk the whole ¼ mile of uphill driveway without stopping twice to huff and puff. And, I'm thinking that if I continue I might even be able to go skiing next season (that's also partly to one more kid off to college so we might be able to even afford a day or two). Upshot is, think of all the stuff you used to do. Wouldn't it be cool to be able to do it again? Fine. Go get in an exercise program—there will be one at your local hospital or gym—because you'll be much more likely to actually do it than if you go it alone. Gaining back the independence you had before is worth the little bit of sweat and dollars it's going to cost you.

Salads

Adjustable Salad

Get salad stuff, like one of the mixes at the market, though greenleaf, romaine or butter lettuces are nice. Add some kind of meat--leftover beef, salmon, tuna, chicken, goat, yak, possum, whatever. Put odd junk on it like diced squash or corn or gar-*BAN*-zo beans (actually the gar-*BAN*-zo beans aren't really that odd in a salad, but doesn't it taste good when you say the word gar-*BAN*-zo?), and/or some kind of fruit. Put on coupons, uh I mean croutons, the low fat/low salt sort. Put on seeds or nuts or some other crunchy thing, crumbled up rice cakes maybe or dried ants or something. Add dressing--if you are allowing the kids to cheat on the heart healthy diet let 'em pick from the stuff at the supermarket--if you are weak and a wuss and can't have any of that stuff around without cheating, keep lots and lots of balsamic vinegar around and just use it straight. At any rate, no matter what the kids do, YOU use the balsamic vinegar straight. You can serve this with other stuff like soups and sandwiches or it can stand alone. 'Speriment with your own variations like taco meat or Chinese veggies or teriyaki whatever (watch for lots of sodium in both of those). Don't use those fried Chinese noodles, tons of salt, fat and other noxious junk. Have fun, be artistic and sleep well.

"Hey!" You say, "There's no ingredient list!" Yeah, so? I do give you some credit for independent thought, so get your scratch pad and write your own. Geez. Some people.

This Space for Notes, Other Recipes, Magical Spells or Whatnot:
Note: This notice will not be repeated, you're just going to have to remember why the back of each page is blank. Can't remember? Ask the local witch doctor what herbs to take for poor memory. Failing that, just get over it. Now quit messing about, turn the page and cook something. Go on!

Red, White and Blue Potato Salad
Baked for your gastric enjoyment

Ok, well so it's not all that obvious, you gotta use a little imagination on this one, ok? You see, there's white potatoes, red kidney beans and black beans which are actually really, really, really dark blue. See? It's all there, red, white and blue! Anyway, it tastes pretty good on a nice summer day along with some barbecued something or other and a tall frosty thingie.

Get all this:

10 pounds potatoes, either red, gold or white, no russets, thank you very much	Dill
One red onion	Garlic powder
1 can kidney beans, unsalted	Black pepper
1 can black beans, unsalted	Olive oil
Mayonnaise, try cutting by 1/3 with non-fat yogurt	1 box eggbeaters
	Lemon juice
Deli mustard with the big chunks of stuff	Baking soda

Do all this: Wash the potatoes, scrub 'em good with a brush, then cut 'em into ½" cubes—Hey! What do you think you're doing?! Don't peel those taters! The peel is where all the vitamins and stuff's at. Just stop it. Now!-- dumping the cubes all the while onto a big baking sheet you've cleverly sprayed with Pam. After all the potatoes are on the sheet and cut up, spray with Pam or better yet olive oil Pam. When that's all done, put the baking sheet in the oven at 375 and cook about 40 minutes or until they're golden brown on the outside and still soft inside. Mmmm. But wait! I said the potatoes were brown. Hmm. Well I said you're gonna have to use your imagination so get with it. <sigh>

While they're cooking take the beans and open the cans but don't take the lids all the way off, prop the cans uppside down (as my kids said when they were little) in the sink and let all the liquid drain out. When they're all drained, rinse with water. Then get out your food processor or blender and put in the eggbeaters, about ¼ cup of lemon juice, three or four tablespoons of mustard, one tablespoon of dill, one tablespoon garlic powder, ½ tablespoon black pepper, a pinch of baking soda and turn the thing on. While it's frantically whirling around, ever so slowly pour about 1/2 cup of extra virgin olive oil into the mix. Let it run for a bit. Stop it. Taste. Fiddle with the seasoning, this ain't science here, it's cooking, ok? Add 1/2 cup prepared mayonnaise, and blend some more. Blend some more. Taste and adjust the spices to your liking and set aside. If it's bitter, add a bit more baking soda and blend some more.

Peel and dice the onion pretty small, say ¼ " or smaller bits, set aside. Oh, by the way, if you have kids that won't eat onions or anything with onions, try adding the onions to the dressing, the final product needs the flavor and they'll never know they are there.

By now your 'taters should be done, so pull the baking sheet and let 'em get cool. Then dump the taters into a big bowl or better yet tupperware thing and add all the other stuff a little at time—you don't want it to be too goopy, so go easy and remember that the more goop you add the higher the fat content. Stir a while, cover and put in the fridge. No matter how hungry you are and how good the tasting went, don't you even think of eating this stuff until tomorrow. As us master chefs say, all the flavors must marry, mellow and meld into a mellifluous mass prior to mastication (that would be chewing to you, Rob). Have some of the dressing left over in case the 'taters soak up too much and leave it dry. A nice semi-dry white wine goes well with this, but then again so does beer, or if you're non-alcoholic cream soda is good. Happy Fourth of July or whatever.

Southwest Salad Dressing
With which you can cleverly make salad,
Coleslaw, fish tacos, or what have you.

This whole thing got started when I was casting about for some clever way of making tuna tacos a little different than the run of the mill lettuce-cheese-tomato approach, so I made this stuff and built some coleslaw. Meanwhile back at the ranch or rather without the ranch dressing, I made a taco salad with it. Then a fajita salad, then a green salad. Then I filled the bathtub with the stuff and took a bath. I was pretty greasy for a while but smelled great.

Quick! Run out and get all this:
Mayonnaise
Fat free sour cream
Fat free plain yogurt
Salt free ketchup
Low salt salsa, Tascosa, Santa Fe are good 'uns
Lemon juice
Cumin
Coriander
Cilantro
Cholula hot sauce
Baking soda

Now do this:
Get a mixing bowl and dump about 1 cup mayo, 1 cup sour cream, 1 cup yogurt, 2 tablespoons each of cumin, coriander and cilantro, 1 cup salsa, 2 tablespoons lemon juice, a good squirt of Cholula, a pinch of baking soda and about ½ cup ketchup. Mix it all together with a whisk and stick it in the icebox. When it's been in there at least 15 minutes, half an hour would be better, taste, adjust seasoning and dress something. No clue what to dress? Well, your kids would likely be upset if you dressed them with this stuff, but if you turn the page, I'll help you out.

Southwest Coleslaw

Make the dressing like I just told you. No, not like that, go back and read the recipe all the way through before you start. There. That's better. This is a tough one so pay attention.

Get this:
Southwest Salad Dressing. I told you, it's on the previous page. <sigh>
1 head of cabbage

Take the head of cabbage. Slice it really thin. Put in a stainless mixing bowl. Add some dressing, about half of what you think you need. Stir. Refrigerate for half an hour. Check. If it's just goopy enough you can serve it. If it's too dry, add about half the dressing you think it needs and stir. If it's too goopy, go get another head of cabbage, slice thin and add some goop. Like I said, it's really tough.

Southwest Taco Salad

Make the dressing like I just told you. No, not like that, go back and read the recipe all the way through before you start. There. That's better.
Get all this stuff and get it right now!

1 package of salad greens
1 package taco cheese
1 jar salsa, low salt, say under 100mg per 2 tbls
1 tub no fat sour cream
1 bag low/no salt tortilla chips,
Some leftover fajitas, taco meat, tuna or what have you.

Now do all this:
Put a handful of chips on a plate. Scatter a handful of greens over that, put a good-sized dollop of meat in the middle. Put a spoonful of sour cream on the meat. Drizzle some dressing around the meat on the greens. Put a couple spoons of salsa over the whole mess. Serve. You could add tomatoes, onions, celery or whatnot. Be creative. Oh, don't forget, a glass of red wine is good for you.

Soups, Stews and Stewps

Non-Heart Attacking Beef Barley Soup

You could do this with chicken stock too. Or vegetable stock, or fish stock or, well, whatever sort of stock you have laying around. Except for maybe rolling stock. Or publicly held stock. Anyway, make sure you make the toast, even if you have to go buy bread to do it, 'cause kids need some distraction from a low salt meal, silly little twits.

Couple soup bones or three quarts of no fat, no sodium commercial beef broth
Celery, whole stalk
Small bag baby carrots
4 or 5 medium potatoes, red, white or gold, not russets
Onion powder
Chopped garlic
Basil, Thyme, Rosemary, Cilantro
Optional: some sort of meat
Not a whole helluva lot of salt

Get a couple soup bones, boil in about 4 or 5 quarts of water for a while. Fish out bones, refrigerate, skim off fat, cut the meat off the bones, chop up about bite size and leave on a plate on the counter. In a couple days it'll dry out and the dogs will love the bits as treats since they'll be pretty tasteless to a human and you don't want to eat 'em. Return pot to stove and reduce until you have about three quarts. Add celery, carrots, potatoes, all diced, and 1 1/2-cup barley. Bring to boil, reduce heat to simmer and cook until veggies tender. At this point you can add meat remembering that your fat content goes way up if you do (from about 4 g total per serving to 16 or 17)--the first time had Italian meatballs (made with ground oatmeal, lean ground beef, Italian spices and eggbeaters), but you could use just about anything laying around the fridge or whatever roadkill you found on your way home. Or you could serve it up without meat, but you have to spice it--add dried basil, thyme, rosemary, and cilantro. Use about 2 tbls each--since you're adding little or no salt you have to really pump the herbs. Add 2 tbls chopped garlic. Add about 6 tbls onion powder--you could use fresh onions, but Mickey won't eat them so I use the powder. I buy it by the 55-gallon drum. Add 1 tbl salt max, or none if you can stand it That's still not much for about 4 qts of soup and the kids actually ate it without adding salt (except for Eiko, who salts breakfast cereal, well, almost. . . Germans. . .) It's important that you add the spices at the end, otherwise the 'taters and barley will absorb all the flavors and everyone will dump entire salt shakers on the stuff to compensate. Find all the leftover hot dog and hamburger buns you have (since there's 6 of us, we always have a few) margarine with Benecol or Smart Choice add garlic powder and parmesan and toast.

Beef Stew al Sudoeste
con Poco Salado y Gordo

(Beef Stew of the Southwest with Little Salt and Fat)

Everybody knows how to make beef stew, right? Ah, well, ok, I've had some that was uh, not quite up to Dinty Moore's standards, but by and large it's a pretty simple dish. But lots of times beef stew gets kinda boring, so we'll fix that today. Lots of times homemade or even prepared beef stew is also really heavy on both fat and salt. We'll fix that today too. Other than spices, the big trick to this recipe is masa flour instead of white flour. If that doesn't mean anything to you, it's ok, I'll explain later.

Stuff to get:
A couple pounds of beef	Rosemary
About 4 cups of carrots	Basil
About the same of celery	Cilantro
About six or eight small red potatoes	Cumin
One large russet potato	Liquid woodsmoke
One medium yellow onion	Chicken broth, no fat, low sodium
Olive oil	Seasoned pepper
Masa (tortilla) flour	Cholula hot sauce
Thyme	Garlic powder

Get a fair sized stock pot and put 2 tbls olive oil in, then put it on the stove on about medium heat. Get the onion, peel it then chop it in about 1/2 inch chunks. When the oil's hot crank the heat up to about 3/4 and dump in the onions, keep an eye on 'em and if they start to brown or stick add some chicken stock. While that's happening, gather up the beef and slice and chop and stuff until it's all in about 1" cubes. Make sure you trim all the visible fat. Gather up all the veggies and do the same, about 3/4" chunks. If you chop up the potatoes at this time, put 'em in a mixing bowl or something and cover 'em with water so they don't turn black. For some reason, my kids won't eat black potatoes. Go figure.

Go check the onions, if they're nearly clear, then dump the meat in, if not; cook 'em a bit longer first. - Interesting aside: My dad always said that if you sauté the onions before putting them in a stew or whatnot, they wouldn't go sour in the fridge. I've never had any go sour so I guess it works.

Back to work. While the meat's cooking, add about a tablespoon each of the spices, a bit more basil and cumin, a couple squirts of woodsmoke, a couple good shakes of garlic, about two tablespoons of seasoned pepper and a couple squirts of hot sauce. Stir. When the meat's mostly cooked, get the masa flour out and sprinkle it over the top of the meat and onions, until everything is mostly covered with flour. Stir. You'll now have this kinda gross looking pasty/lumpy stuff that smells pretty good. Now dump the chicken broth over the whole mess and stir. Add the veggies and stir some more. Stir. Bring to a boil and stir. After it's boiling reduce the heat to low and simmer until the potatoes are done. Leave it in the pot, take it off the heat, let it cool and stick the pot in the fridge. Hah! Thought you were gonna get to eat it tonight dincha! Well, you can't. It'll be better tomorrow anyway, so go make some PBJ for tonight. Goes good with sourdough toast. Ya know, it occurs to me you could add some green chili to this too, that's very sudoeste, and it'd go good in there too. Try it and let me know how it worked out.

Oh, yeah. Masa flour is what tortillas are made from. You could make some out of the flour if you want. There's instructions on the bag. Me, I'll just buy tortillas but masa flour is also is a dandy thickener for most anything, especially if you want it to be kinda southwestern. It gives the stew a golden color and an earthy, semi-corn-sweet kinda flavor. Good stuff. If you don't have masa flour you can reverse engineer it by tearing up tortillas and cooking them down to nothing. That's how they built the Stealth fighter out of UFOs.

Fat Jack's Original Chili goes to the Gym for some fat loss...

This is an old family recipe handed down through the men in the White family for 5 generations. NOT. I got tired of buying Carroll Shelby's Chili Fixin's so I swiped the ingredient list and 'sperimented till I got it right. Which is to say, a helluva lot better than Carroll Shelby ever done or anybody else for that matter. I used to add Jack Daniels but then I realized it tasted like s**! so I quit pourin' it in the pot. Now I pour the JD in me while I'm cookin'. Helps take the edge off when the kids help. I gotta tell you, this one is a regular pain in the posterior to make low fat. But I did!

Ingredients:
About 2-3 pounds ground beef
1 purple onion
1 yellow onion
Masa (tortilla) flour
Garlic
Seasoned pepper
Wright's wood smoke
Cumin
Coriander

Cilantro
Cholula hot sauce
Olive oil
1 can no salt diced tomatoes
3 or 4 Jalapeno peppers
2 cans no salt tomato sauce, 12-oz. Maybe. One could be enough. Use your best judgement, but remember this is known as "a bowl of red."

How to do it:
Take ground beef and set it on the counter. Make into big ol' burgers about a pound each. Take 'em out to the barbecue and grill 'em until medium well done. Bring 'em back into the house. You see, when you do that, most of the fat hits the coals or the gas burners so you reduce the fat by a whole bunch, say to about 6 grams saturated per serving. Not bad, eh? Take a purple and a yellow onion, peel and dice about ¼ ". Dump some olive oil, 'bout 2 tbls in your stock pot and sauté the onions. When the onions are clear, dump in the beef and bust it up. When the meat is brown dump in the tomato sauce and tomatoes, add the spices as follows:
1 tablespoon of garlic, 4 or 5 table spoons of cumin, ½ that amount of Coriander, 1 tablespoon of cilantro, 2 to 4 capfuls of woodsmoke, a tablespoon of seasoned pepper, about 6-200 table spoons of hot sauce-- The amount of hot sauce depends on how hot you want it and you want it kinda hot, this is authentic by-God-Texas (put your hand over your heart) chili, not that Mexican goulash that has beans and soy protein you can get toy poodles to eat. That said, all these amounts are subject to change based on how you like this stuff to taste. I never make it the same way twice in a row, but it's always good and this is a good starting place.

Simmer the whole wretched mess, at least 20-min, but it will be better the longer you cook it. Stir occasionally. Soon as you set it to simmer, mix about 1 cup of masa flour in a 16 oz glass of water—beat it with a fork. Leave the fork in it, so you can find it later, and set the flour and water mixture in the fridge. When it's simmered as much as you can stand, stir in the flour and water. Simmer for at least a ½ hour, again, the longer the better. For best results, take the pot off the stove, allow to cool and place in the fridge for a couple of days. If you want to get all medieval about the fat, you can peel what's there off the top when you pull it out of the fridge. Reheat and eat with sourdough bread. If you have to, you can eat it out of the pot the day you make it but, like stew, it will be better the second day.

Clam Chowder Just as filling, but less fat

In the wintertime a little clam chowder is good for the soul. The guts too. You'll note that this recipe has no onions. This is because when I put onions in nearly anything, my kids take to wailing, gnashing of teeth, wearing sackcloth and ashes and other subtle means of peaceful protest. So, if you want, add about one onion diced small, sauté it first. Or you can be sneaky like me and add onion powder. Remember that if you're gonna cook without salt, then you're gonna have to pump the other spices, so take these amounts as a starting place and use your clever little tongue to get the spices right.

Get this stuff:
4 cans diced clams, drained
6 or so medium red or white potatoes, Yukon golds are good too
4 cans condensed skim milk, unsweetened
¼ cup Smart Balance margarine or the equivalent—read the label
¼ cup packaged bacon bits—the real ones, those soy bean fake things will dissolve in the soup and mutate into something unpleasant and the real ones are only 1.5g fat per tbls.
1 bay leaf
2 tbls Onion powder
1 tbls lemon juice
2 tbls Sriracha hot sauce
Pepper to taste—use white pepper, it's prettier and tastes the same as black
1 pinch of garlic powder
1 tsp liquid woodsmoke
1/3 cup white flour

Do all this:
Peel the potatoes, boil till cooked in water, cool and slice in ½" cubes. In a stockpot, dump the clams, drain and remove from can first please, margarine and milk, save about a cup for a secret mission later. Heat on medium. Add the potatoes and if the milk doesn't cover add some more. Add everything else on the list above except the bacon bits and anything else you think would go in this—no, beer will not work in this soup. Now take the milk you saved put it in a large glass and add the flour. Stir briskly with a fork until it makes a smooth paste the consistency of, uh, maple syrup? No, that's not it. Uh, the consistency of uh, cream gravy, that's it! Then dump it into the soup and stir. Stir some more. Then, stir. Cook the whole wretched mess about a couple hours on a very low simmer. Ladle a bit into some bowls and sprinkle some bacon bit on top, not many, salt and fat you know. It's nice to crumble up some saltines into it. Ritz are good too. Not many though, unless they're the low salt variety. Serve with a nice unpretentious white wine or a bottle of Coors. Or a glass or water. Oh, and make sure you give the folks a spoon. You know, if you could find a nice small round sourdough loaf you could bread-bowl it. . . Just a thought.

Crawdad Jambalaya

I'm given to understand that those little fresh water lobsters are properly called "crayfish." Nonsense! Any fool can see they aren't fish! 'Sides, when I was a kid they were crawdads and I've received no notice of a change. That settled, here's what you do.

Get all this stuff:

2 pounds of crawdads
1 pound shrimp (optional)
1 pound of chicken breasts
1 pound turkey bratwurst
3 large bell peppers, assorted colors
1 onion
2 boxes sliced mushrooms
4 or 5 cloves garlic chopped fine

2 quarts or so low sodium no fat chicken stock
(or shrimp or crawdad stock)
Smart Balance margarine or equivalent
Flour
Emeril's essence
Sriracha hot sauce
Pepper

Do all this:
Get the crawdads. Now that sounds simple but there's ways and there's ways. You can get 'em frozen in the super market, that's the easiest way, or you can have the kids go catch a mess of 'em. If you do the latter, be sure to put 'em in a bucket of clean water for at least a day, two would be better, to clean 'em out. Then boil 'em till they turn red, allow to cool and peel 'em. (Save the shells! Freeze 'em and boil 'em later for about 20 minutes or so to make crawdad stock to replace the chicken broth next time you make this, works with shrimp shells too). If you got the frozen ones, defrost 'em. Cut chicken breast in about ¾" chunks and toss it in with the sausage you're slicing up in about the same size chunks. Toss it where you ask? In the stock pot of course, with about two tbls of canola oil set on high heat, for as long as it takes for the chicken to cook through or the sausage to brown if it starts to stick, add a bit of the stock to unstick it. Remove from the pot when brown, leaving the oil and whatnot behind. Dump in about 2 tbls margarine and reduce heat to medium. Dump in the garlic, mushrooms, onion and bell peppers that you already diced up, no seeds, about ½" chunks and sauté for four or five minutes. Add some stock if it starts to stick. Oh, add a couple cranks of the pepper mill, and three tablespoons of essence when you start this stuff. Remove from pot, leaving the liquids in the pot. Take about ½ to 1 cup of flour and dump in the pot, cook for about 4 or 5 minutes on high, add some stock if it gets chunky or more flour if it's loose, you want it to be about the same consistency at 90 weight gear oil. When it's blonde, it's done, though it may be of dubious intelligence. Now, dump in the stock, the meat and the veggies. Squirt in about two to four tablespoons of hot sauce (or to taste if you're either a wuss or double tough). Bring to boil. Reduce heat to medium low and cook for fifteen or twenty minutes. Remove from heat. Oh, yeah, as always, when you think you're about done cooking this stuff, taste it and adjust seasonings, also, if you can't manage crawdads, shrimp will work, as will hot Italian turkey sausage if you can't find bratwurst. Go make room in the fridge and stick the whole pot in there. Wait until dinnertime tomorrow, and then cook a couple cups of rice, while you put the goop from yesterday on to heat. Put about a half cup of cooked rice in a bowl; ladle on some of the goop on, being careful to get some of all the ingredients in each bowl. Open a bottle of red wine, play zydeco music, eat and drink. Go to bed early, you have a busy day tomorrow.

Pepper Pot Soup without all the baggage

When I first came up with this recipe, I actually said, "Whatever you do, don't dump off the grease, how the heck are you gonna keep your cholesterol count up if you do that?!" Well, I kept my cholesterol level up, and then after two heart attacks, I spent a total of six days in the hospital, got two stents, and some serious medical bills. So, it seems to me a few changes are in order, doncha think?

Great stuff when you have a head cold. Guaranteed to clear your sinus if you add enough hot sauce. Now that I think of it, it's darn good even if you don't have a cold. . .

Ingredients:
2# turkey sausage smoked, Polish if you can get it. Hot Italian turkey sausage would work as would just plain smoked sausage.
1 each, green, yellow and red bell peppers, or all one color if you can't find t'others.
2 12oz can diced tomatoes unsalted or you could use about 6 medium fresh ones
1 med/large onion, yellow is nice
Seasoned pepper
Garlic
Wright's wood smoke
Sriracha hot sauce
Smart Balance margarine or equivalent
Tarragon
Thyme
Red wine
Flour
Water
Rice

Do all this:
Cube the sausage, ½", Cube the peppers, ½", dice the onion, ½". then put about two tbls margarine in a stockpot. Saute the peppers and onions, add a bit of chicken stock if they start to stick. If you're feeling froggy, hop on down to the Grocery Store and get some jalapeno and serrano peppers and cook those with the rest. If you're truly manly use habanero or scotch bonnets. I don't, I'm just not that tough. Sorry.

Anyway, then dump in the sausage, about a tablespoon each of all the spices, add about 1--200 tbls of Sriracha to taste depending on how hot you want it. More than what you got there, doggone it, this *IS* a pepper pot you know! Add two or three good squirts of woodsmoke and about half a bottle of good red wine, add the tomatoes and add water to cover the sausage and veggies. Simmer for a bit, say half an hour. When you've put it to simmer, mix about a cup and a half of flour with water in a 16 oz glass, beat with a fork and put it in the fridge till the simmerin' is done--this is a way cool trick that will prevent lumps in the mixtures. I invented it, of course. Now, get a glass of that wine or a couple shots of JD if it's been a rough day, and go watch <u>Friends</u> on TV for a while.

When you are tired of simmering and watching TV, dump the flour and water mixture into the pot. Add a couple of cups of water if you need to, until you have roughly the same amount of broth as you do lumpy pepper and meat stuff. Check the seasoning, alter to taste. Simmer for a couple of hours or until your wife gets home. Fill the bowls about half full of rice, then dump the soup over it. Like all soups and stews, it's better if it ages in the fridge a day or two, plus you can skim the hardened fat off it if there is any. This stuff is really good with garlic/parmesan toast. Make this when you have a cold, and your sinus will clear right up. Then again, make this when you don't have a cold and maybe you won't get one.

Low Fat Fungus Among Us Ragout.

So I thought to myself since the kids don't like mushrooms, I ought to go get some and make a ragout.

Stuff:
About 2 # of turkey, chicken, lean pork or beef, or maybe squid, though that last might be a stretch. Or, you could use some turkey sausage. I'd stay away from tofu for this one. . .
A large onion
About 30 each, shitake, brown and white mushrooms or whatever you can get
1 12oz can of unsalted diced tomatoes
Garlic
Seasoned pepper
Worcestershire
Sriracha hot sauce
Liquid smoke
Red wine
12 oz low sodium chicken broth
Flour
Olive oil

Dump 2 tbls olive oil into stockpot on high heat, dice onion small and sauté until clear, add a little chicken broth if it gets too dry. Stir a lot. Slice one kind of mushroom vertically, one kind horizontally, and quarter one kind. That doesn't really make any difference in how the ragout will taste, but you can tell what kind of mushroom you're eating if you do it this way. Dump the mushrooms in and sauté them too, again adding chicken broth as needed. Dump in garlic to taste, I used about 6 cloves, and about 2 tbls of seasoned pepper, about four shakes of hot sauce, 1tsp of liquid smoke and about 2 tbls of Worcestershire. Stir a lot. When the mushrooms get tenderish, dump in a cup or so of whine, uh, sorry, Shannon just came in to talk about Mickey, make that wine. Continue to heat on medium flame.
Stir a lot.

Get a frying pan, start it heating and then quarter the sausage lengthwise, and then slice into 1/4" slices. Dump the meat, previously cubed to about ½" chunks, into the frying pan and brown well in about a tablespoon of olive oil. It impresses guests if you turn the meat bits by doing that wrist-flip thing, but a spoon works too. When the bits are well browned, dump them into the ragout and add about 3/4 of the chicken broth. Dump about a cup of wine into the frying pan, deglaze and dump into the stockpot. Dump the can of tomatoes in. Heat stockpot on low flame.

Take the rest of the broth and put it in a large glass. Add about 4 tbls of white flour. Mix with a fork. Yes, it has to be a fork, this is no time to be getting kinky. Put the glass in the 'fridge. Heat the pot of fungus for about an hour or two, stirring a lot, about a half hour in get the glass out of the fridge, stir it and dump the flour/broth mixture in. Cook for another half-hour or so.

Cook some rice. Serve the rice in a bowl, ladle the fungus ragout over the rice. Drink the leftover wine with it. Make this toast, *"Thou hast brought a Fungus Amongus, Ole!"*

Irish Stew

What's the matter bunky? Ya say Bayfield Sheep Trailin' and Heritage Day is comin' and ya got no good mutton recipes? Ya say all yer friends and neighbors, as well as yer dear and lovin' family say all yer lamb recipes taste like road kill venison? Well . . .

PULL UP YER PANTS AND SHOUT "SAINT'S BE PRAISED!" 'CAUSE I GOT ALL YER PROBLEMS SOLVED RIGHT HERE AN' NOW!

Quick like, run out and get all this stuff:
A bunch of potatoes, red, white or Yukon gold. Don't get russets. Get say, ten pounds.
A bunch of turnips. About half as many as you got potatoes.
About 3 good sized white or yellow onions
About 5 pounds of lamb roast, boneless unless you really want to bone it.
Canola oil
White pepper
Water

Put on your pinafore and do all this:
Peel and dice the onions, sauté' in about 2 tbls canola oil, set aside. Then fish through the potatoes for the biggest ones, and pick out as many as you have people in your family. Hide these in a dark cool place, 'cause you're gonna use them for some other dinner some other time and you're gonna bake 'em, but that's another story so forget about that, quit distracting me and we'll cook some stew.

Take half the potatoes, peel 'em. Dump 'em in a big honkin' stock pot with enough water to cover. Boil, covered for a long time. When they potatoes are boiled down to very very soft, get an old fashioned potato masher, you know, one of those wire squiggly looking things, and mash the potatoes. Add water so they're really, really soupy. Peel all the rest of the potatoes, as well as the turnips. I know, I know. "I hate turnips," you whine. Well tough, you gotta have 'em and they'll really mellow in the cooking process so do it anyway. If you don't like the finished product, you can go to McDonald's and get a side salad, ok?

Cube the potatoes and the turnips in exactly ¾" cubes. Get the tape and measure if you have to. Ok, ok, they can vary a little, say +/- .003". Get the lamb, bone it if you decided you needed that particular complication in your life, cube it the same size as the praties (Irish for potatoes) and the turnips, but you can vary the size a little more as meat is squishier than veggies. Ok, dump the taters, turnips and meat and those sautéed onions you probably put somewhere you can't remember into the stockpot, make sure the whole wretched mess is covered with water. Bring to boil, reduce to low and simmer until meat is cooked through.

Ok, I know what you're thinking. "He didn't brown the meat!" That's one of the many cool things about this dish. You don't hafta brown the meat. You don't hafta add flour or other thickening 'cause the boiled down taters do that. You do have to add a wee bit 'o salt (*wee bit, lad!*), white pepper to taste just before you serve it, which will be when the meat is tender and cooked through.   Don't season before this 'cause the taters will suck up about seven thousand pounds of salt and I'm told and we all now know tha' t'ain't good for you and far be it from me to make y'all sick. Serve with soda scones. I'd tell you how to make those but I've no idea so go find some old Irishwoman to teach you how. If that doesn't work, try sourdough bread, and if you really want to wow the masses, make sourdough bread bowls and dump it in that. See you at the park!

Corn Chowder

Well, I was sitting around the house one day, trying to come up with something for dinner. I thought I'd make T-bones with corn and some potatoes. Imagine my surprise when I discovered we had no meat!! Yikes! Could this happen in my house? No! Well, ok so it did. Anyway, I had the taters and the corn and the rest is history.

1 quart cooked corn, niblitized
1½ quarts diced red potatoes
2 cups diced carrots
2 quarts low or no sodium chicken broth
4 cans condensed skim milk
¼ cup Smart Balance margarine or equivalent—read the label
Flour
Tarragon
Seasoned pepper
Cayenne

Do all this:
Melt margarine in large stockpot. When melted, add enough flour to make a thick white roux, you're looking for about 90-weight gear oil. If you don't know how thick that is, go find some old gear-head to tell you, or better show you. Cook a while, but don't brown. Add potatoes, corn, carrots, chicken broth, and bring to boil. Reduce heat to fast simmer and add milk. Wait about ten minutes then add all spices (go easy and taste a lot, this is easy to over-do) to taste. Cook until potatoes are tender. Serve with an unpretentious beer, say Coors and sourdough bread, but make sure it's really good, actually sour bread. Eat. Clear table, get someone else to do dishes, and make sure they remember to run the damned dishwasher. And don't feed the leftovers to the cat, they'll be even better for lunch tomorrow.

Semi-easy Homebuilt Chicken Soup

You remember when grammaw used to make soup and that was pretty doggone good. But chasin' that chicken around the yard, getting it plucked and prepped and roasted was a pain. So try this: Run on down to the super market and get one of those roasted chickens they have on that whirligig roaster thing. Be careful and don't get an oddly flavored one like cilantro lime or lemon pepper or something (I did this once and it made some really odd tasting soup). Just get the standard roast chicken.

Then, get all this stuff:
1 pound peeled baby carrots
1 pound celery
1 large purple onion
1 large bag extra wide egg noodles
1 can chicken broth no fat, low salt
Tarragon
Olive oil

Take it all home. Let it cool. Now, do all this: Get a large stock pot, a smaller stock pot, a cutting board, a medium size stainless steel mixing bowl, a big ol' chef's knife, a large colander and a stove. Take the chicken and pull off all the skin. Feed 2/3 of the skin to the dog and take the rest out back and feed to the barn cats. Pull off the legs and wings. Pull the meat off the legs and as much as you can get off the wings, tear it into pieces no longer than an inch, inch and a half at most and toss it into the mixing bowl. Toss the bones into the large stockpot. Pull all the meat from the carcass and tear it up as above. This is very therapeutic if you visualize the right people, animals, devices, cars or tractors. When you have all the meat off the carcass, legs and wings, and all the bones in the pot, then add water to the pot to cover the bones. Put it on the stove, cover and let it simmer at medium low for several hours. Say 3 to 5. Longer is better, but keep an eye on the liquid level, you want to cook it down but not boil it dry. Put the chicken, carrots and celery in the 'fridge. Go watch some TV, or do a tune up on the Jeep or run to town for the mail you forgot to get when you got all the ingredients.

About an hour before dinner, do all this: Take the colander and put it over the smaller stockpot, dump the broth into it and filter out all the bones. Put the bones in the bag the chicken came with and throw 'em out. Don't feed 'em to the dog or cat, not good for 'em I'm told. Put the small stockpot on the stove on medium low, say 3 1/2 out of 10 if you have an electric. Dump in the chicken. Get out a half pound of carrots, slice 'em in half, something less than an inch long and put 'em in the mixing bowl you used for the chicken. Use the leftovers to snack on while you're messing with the rest of this stuff. Dump the carrots in the broth. Dump in the canned chicken broth. Add about one tablespoon of dried tarragon and some fresh ground pepper to taste, cover. Put two tbls olive oil in a sauté pan. Dice the onion. Cry. Put the onion in the sauté pan and cook until clear. Dump the whole mess into the broth. Wait ten minutes. Stand in the kitchen tapping your foot impatiently while you wait. Clean off the celery, whack off the gunky ends and slice into about ½" long chunks, you'll want about six stalks. Dump 'em in the broth. Once you've got all that stuff in there, make sure it's all covered by the broth add stock if not. Take the big stockpot you cooked the bones in and make sure all the bones are gone, but don't rinse it out and add about two quarts of water. Bring to boil. Add the noodles and cook like they say to do it on the package. Drain in the cleaned out colander and return to pot with 2 tbls olive oil to keep 'em from sticking to each other. Set aside. Cook the broth until the carrots are tender. Get some bowls, fill about half full of noodles then ladle soup over them, stir. You see, for years I tried to cook the noodles or rice along with the broth and it always ended up mush, then I tried cooking them separately and it worked splendidly. Serve with parmesan toast and a semi dry white wine. Or beer, everything goes with beer. If you're gonna save some for later, store the broth and noodles separately and you won't mush out. This also works for rice soups. Duh. Anyway, it was semi-easy, wasn't it? Pretty good eatin' too.

Entrées, Sides and Everything else that Isn't Soup, Salad or Dessert

Carne Asada del Gringo Gordo con Arroz y Frijoles

OK, so I went to the Dolores Diner, I think, in Dolores, Colorado and got some Carne Asado. The beans and rice were ok, but the meat was terrific. Speaking remarkably ineffective fifth-grade Spanish rewarded me with directions to the bathroom, another glass of water and the knowledge that *pajaro* means "bird" and not "duck, which is *pato*. Sadly, my *Espanol* did not elicit any understandable recipes. So, I went 'head on and made up my own, hence the title. So, anyway, here's what you do:

Get this stuff:
Some meat. The stuff in the restaurant was flank steak and was tender, but when I made it the first time with flank steak it was every bit as tender as your average latigo. So, if you're gonna use that, beat on it with one of those little hammers with the pointy things on it. Or marinate it in something acidic. Vinegar or lemon juice or something. Since you're gonna season each piece separately get as much as you want. Leftovers make great sandwiches.

2 cans frijoles refritos (that's refried beans to non-linguists) check labels and get lowest fat	Cumin
	Coriander
2 cups rice uncooked	Cilantro
12 oz V8 Juice, low sodium	Ancho chili powder
1 can low sodium/fat chicken broth	Garlic powder
1 can diced tomatoes unsalted	Cholula brand hot sauce
Nacho/Taco shredded cheese—the real stuff, 'cause the low fat stuff tastes like wax	Liquid smoke

Do all this long before you're going to eat, say the day, or morning before:
Get the meat out and beat it if you got that kind of meat. If you got the 'tother kind of meat just lay it out on a plate in one layer. Put a dollop (technical term—about ¼ tsp) of liquid smoke on each piece. Sprinkle each piece with cumin, coriander, garlic powder, ancho chili powder (you can substitute cayenne if you don't have it, but it'll be better with ancho), and some salt. Rub it in. Turn the pieces and repeat. Cover plate with tinfoil (ok, I know, it's aluminum now, but I'm old, ok?) and stick it in the fridge.

Do all this just before you're going to eat:
Open both cans of frijoles refritos and dump 'em in a sauce pot—clever trick to get all the beans out of the can, take a knife and poke a hole in the bottom of the can, then holding the can over the sauce pan, blow through the hole, the beans will come out in one can-shaped chunk—heat them covered on low, or maybe two if your knobs have numbers. Take another fairly large saucepan and dump the broth, V8 and diced tomatoes in. Dump in ½ tsp cumin, ¼ tsp coriander, 1 tsp garlic powder, ¼ tsp ancho chili powder, 1 tbl Cholula. Heat to a boil, stir a bit. Dump in the two cups of rice, cook for about 15 minutes or until the rice is done which will be in about 15 minutes or so. Stir the beans while this is going on. Take the meat out of the fridge and fry it—use about two tablespoons of olive oil to start, then add ¼ cup of chicken broth when it's going good--on medium high or about seven or eight if you've number knobs. Won't take long to cook, maybe four or five minutes a side. You could also do this on the grill, but I haven't tried that yet, I'm outta propane. By the time you're done doing all that the beans and rice should be done, so slap a bit of each on the plates, stick some cheese on the beans, maybe a dab or two on the steaks as well, garnish with a little fresh cilantro and eat it up. Best with a nice Mexican beer like Pacifico.

Something Close to Chicken Marsala with Catholic Chicken

You know how it goes, you decide to have something Italian so you go check the Italian section of Betty Crocker, Joy of Cooking and Fannie Farmer. You read the directions, ingredients and so forth. And you say to yourself, "Jeez, I don't have time to read all this, it's cutting into strawberry daiquiri time!" So, you cast another brief glance at the ingredient list and sally forth to the pantry. Hmm. Got chicken, got tomato sauce, got marsala, got garlic, got pasta, got hot sauce. Should be good to go. Now I know you might not be as well prepared as I am so go get all this stuff if you aren't:

As many chicken breasts as people to feed.
Pasta, I used rotini
Asparagus, broccoli, zucchini or something green
Two packages sliced mushrooms
One each red and green bell pepper
One bottle marsala
Garlic, fresh or powdered

Onion, fresh or powdered
One can tomato sauce
Low or no fat *Zesty* Italian salad dressing
Cholula hot sauce
Liquid smoke
Olive oil
Red wine vinegar

First. Get the chicken and toss it into a bowl of some sort. Dump in enough Zesty Italian dressing to cover and leave it for at least half an hour. You've been wondering about the latter half of the title, haven't you? "**Catholic Chicken**?" you say, "What is that? What if I'm Jewish? Do I have to be confirmed to eat it? To cook it?" Well, no, you don't. You see the definition of "catholic" is *universal*. And that's exactly what this chicken is—you can marinate it in the *zesty,* grill it up and use it for almost recipe that calls for chicken. The mix of vinegar and spices is perfectly suited to the meat. So now you know. Onward!

Dice half of each pepper. 'Bout a quarter cup of extra virgin olive oil in a big frying pan. Heat to medium high. Add two squirts of liquid smoke. Add about four squirts of hot sauce. Add two tablespoons garlic powder and about the same amount of onion powder. Why not fresh you ask? Well you see my kids are very sensitive about what they eat, so if there are any visible onion or garlic pieces, they won't even try it. Doesn't matter that it tastes exactly the same. . . <sigh> Toss in the mushrooms and sauté, after a couple minutes add the pepper and half the marsala. Taste it. It should be sweet-ish. If not, add more wine. When the mushrooms look cooked, add one can tomato sauce. Stir, taste and adjust seasonings/wine. Reduce to simmer and ignore for a while.

Cook the pasta per package directions. Or, you could add some oregano to the water along with a squirt of liquid smoke. Or not. Your call, but that's what I did. Oh, buy the way, when you go to drain the pasta if you give the colander a squirt of Pam on both sides, it makes clean up much easier. Also slip about a tablespoon of extra virgin olive oil in the pot when you return the pasta to it, stir a bit and it won't stick together or to the pan.

Fire up the Barbie. When it's hot, slap the chicken on there, cook about 6 or so minutes per side, on low heat. It would be nice if you could get that nice cross hatch branding thing going on, but really cooked is what we're after. When they've been on the grill for a couple minutes pour a bit of the dressing on each. Do the same when you flip 'em.

Nuke the asparagus or what have you for as long as it needs, about 4 – 6 minutes for 'sperigus. I usually make a little sauce for that, ¼ cup olive oil, add ¼ cup red wine vinegar and a table spoon of garlic powder, keep on very low heat and pour over the 'sperigus when you serve 'em. Now. Dump the pasta in the middle of the plate, put a catholic chicken breast on top, ladle some sauce over it, artfully place the asparagus over and around, serve and bask in the adoration of your family and guests.

Carnitas Fajitas

Years ago my wife used to travel for work. She had occasion to go to San Diego quite a lot. There's a restaurant in Old Town down there that serves *carnitas*. I know what you're thinking, "yeah, the little deep fried thingies you mix with loose beans!" WRONG! Carnitas San Diego style are chunks of pork, shredded, spiced and refried. All very well and good but as you know, I can't be accused of stealing recipes since I always change stuff, usually fundamentally. Well, here's what I did: Since it's been so long since she had 'em, and since I never have, I decided to tweak the recipe to fit my own tweaked world view, so,

Get all this:
2+# pork loin
Three bell peppers, assorted colors
   if you can manage it, esthetics you know.
Couple cans of chicken broth
   or say a quart of homemade.
Masa flour
One large yellow onion
Large flour tortillas
Fajita seasoning
Black Pepper

Now, do all this:
Black pepper the pork loins, barbecue or broil until mostly done. Allow to cool, slice in about 1" chunks, dump in crock pot or stew pot if you don't have a crock pot, add chicken broth to cover cook long time until meat falls apart at the touch of a fork. Add about six or so heaping table spoons masa flour, heat to boiling, reduce temp to simmer and add the fajita spices to taste. If you're gonna use all the individual ingredients, all I can tell you is dump stuff in about equal amounts then taste and add a bit of this or that until you get it where it tastes like fajitas. Sorry I can't be more specific, but I got faith in you—after all, you're smart enough to be reading this, no? Meanwhile, back at the ranch, slice all the peppers and onions in exactly 3/8" wide slices. Measure if you have to. Ok, don't, just kidding. Back to the meat—2 tbls olive or canola oil in a skillet, dump in about half of the meat and brown it, adding some chicken stock if it starts to stick, dump into a oven safe dish, and do the same with the rest of the meat. In the same pan, dump in 2 more tbls olive or canola oil, then when it's hot, the onions, adding chicken stock again if they stick. When they start to go clear add the bell peppers, and cook till nearly soft. Add fajita spices to taste and a dash of lemon juice. You can add tequila if you want, but don't worry about it if you drank it all up.
Heat the tortillas, put a dab of meat in the bottom, some pepper-onions on top and serve with beer or red wine. Ole! Oh, by the way, the wife says I didn't nail the San Diego restaurant version, but since she can't tell me what I did wrong she has to suffer with this stuff, which she says is really good anyway.

Curried Beef Balls or Maybe Turkey or Chicken Balls

So, you see, we used to have these two heifers. And after feeding them up pretty good and graining them for a while we had 'em butchered. Now I figured that with some 750 pounds of beef it we'd have steak for years. What we got, and you will too if you raise your own beef, is about 50 pounds of steak and 700 pounds of ground beef. So, to make a long story longer, I've been really stretching to come up with ground beef recipes. This is one of 'em and it has the added attraction of being a make-ahead thingie that you can freeze and use later and stuff.

Drop everything, run out to the Jeep and go get this stuff at the store:

2# ground beef. Of course if you've raised your own, get it out the freezer and de-freeze it. You can substitute ground turkey, chicken or mix half and half, or thirds or whatever to reduce the fat content even more.
Between two and three cups of instant oatmeal.
1 box eggbeaters.
6 tbls hot curry powder.
6 tbls mild curry powder.
6 tbls powdered garlic.
2 tbls Worcestershire sauce.
1 tsp liquid smoke.
Black pepper.

Go heat up the oven to 350 first, cause then you don't have to wait for it. Now get a big mixing bowl and put in the meat. Put the same amount of oatmeal as you have meat. Put in the eggbeaters. Put in the spices, the smoke and the Worcestershire sauce. Get your hands in there and mash it all up together. If you have anger management issues you can use this time to imagine all sorts of nasty things you're doing to the causes of those issues, or you can just watch tv while you're doing it like I do. When the oatmeal and the spices and stuff all look to be pretty evenly distributed, go wash your hands 'cause they're really yucky.

Get a cookie sheet, line it with foil so you won't have to wash it later, you lazy person, you! Then put a rack on it so the meatballs don't stew in a little lake of grease. Get the mixing bowl full of unborn meatballs and set it nearby, then start rolling little beef balls about the size of a ping pong ball, which is slightly smaller than a golf ball, lots smaller than a baseball and nowhere near as big as a football which would be the wrong shape anyway. As you roll the balls, set 'em about a ¼" away from each other and the sides of the pan. While you're doing this it helps to sing traditional East Indian folksongs. If you don't know any of those, just whistle Dixie. When you have 'em all rolled out, stick the pan in the oven for 30 minutes, and take a break. Take 'em out when the dinger dings, and put 'em in some sort of container. I use a small mixing bowl.

Now you've got choices. You can take these things and stick 'em in a ziplock bag and freeze 'em for later use in whatever meatball recipe you have lying around. You can whip up some spaghetti sauce and add 'em for a little different take on 'sketti 'n meatballs. Or, you can do the following:

Cook some noodles, kinda al dente. Toss 'em in a casserole dish. Dump in twenty or so meatballs. Melt about a ¼ cup Smart Balance margarine in a saucepan, add about the same amount of white flour. Add one tbls each of hot and mild curry sauce, add 1 tbls garlic powder. Cook a bit. Add one can low sodium chicken broth, cook till smooth and hot, then pour over the noodles and meatballs, cook in a 350-degree oven for 20 minutes or so and pull it out and eat it.

Eggplant Parmesano de Aintagonnakillya

Ok, you say you can't eat Eye-tal-yun anymore 'cause it's too fattening, and besides since the heart attack you can't have fat, salt or anything else that's good. Well, I'm here to tell ya, it's gonna be ok, we're gonna de-fatify an old Eytie favorite, so quick like, go get all this stuff:

1 medium eggplant sliced
1 box eggbeaters Beaten
   with 2 tablespoons skim milk
Dried Italian bread crumbs
Flour
Olive oil in a sprayer or olive oil Pam
6 ounces tomato paste
6 ounces white or red wine
Pinch dried oregano
Pepper, to taste
1 clove of garlic, crushed
1/2 pound mozzarella, sliced
1 cup freshly grated Parmesan cheese

Preheat oven to 400 degrees F. Slice washed eggplant 1/2-inch thick. Dredge slices in flour, then dip slices into the eggbeaters mixture and then after you've mixed a couple tbls of parmesan into the bread crumbs run the eggplant through that, coat well. Spray a cookie sheet with olive oil. Arrange each slice of coated eggplant in one layer on the cookie sheet and sprayer each piece ever so lightly with olive oil. Bake in the oven for about 15 minutes. Check that the slices are golden brown, turn then and bake for another 15 minutes. They should be golden brown on both sides, 'cause my daddy used to say, "If it's golden brown it's done, if it's black, you're done." Set aside.
Dump the tomato paste and the wine in a saucepan, and add the oregano, pepper, and garlic. Put all the eggplant in a flat casserole dish. Just one layer, 'cause two would be wrong and we don't want to be wrong, right?. Spoon a dab, say 2 tbls of sauce on each slice and hide it with a slice of mozzarella so they won't know we did it (heheheheh) then top with about 1/8" of the sauce. Sprinkle parmesan and grate a bit of the mozzarella on top and slap 'er in the oven, 400, 'member? For about 20 minutes. Serve with a nice Chianti and some crusty italian bread. If you wanna be really fancy, mix some good olive oil with dried oregano and rosemary then whisk in a little balsamic vinegar and dip the bread in it. Might be enough to make you start speaking Italian, paisano!

Fat Jack's Almost Grilled Sandwiches
A favorite of the Bayfield High School Cheerleading Squad—3rd in the State 2007!

I was going to make this rumaki like thing, with roast beef rather than bacon and with artichoke hearts. But the thought of it kept bothering me. I couldn't figure out how to eat 'em. So I slept on it. Then Pat Morita came to me in a dream and begged me not to single handedly destroy Japanese cooking. So I tried a sandwich with water chestnuts and artichoke hearts. Didn't work. So I changed it and came up with this:

Stuff:
Sour dough bread
Some sort of beef roast, trimmed of all fat
Garlic
Parmesan
Mayonnaise, cut the fat by 1/3 by adding 1/3 non-fat yogurt
Smart Balance or equivalent margarine
A-1 sauce
Cholula or Srirachi hot sauce
Italian salad dressing, fat free
Tomatoes
Lettuce

Do this:
Marinate beef overnight in Italian dressing. Fire up the barbie and barbecue the beef for about ten minutes each side on low. Remove from heat when done and slice thin, less than ¼ ".
→ Clever tip #1: If you take the back end, or handle of the ka-dink (spatula to the uninitiated) and mash it into the meat on the grill and if it leaves a depression, the meat's rare. If it doesn't stay mashed down, it's about medium for beef, or done for pork and chicken.
→ Clever tip #2: You know how when you bite into a sandwich and you drag half the filling out onto your chin and shirt and everything and make a big mess? Sucks, doesn't it? Try this: Slice the beef into little strips across the grain then put the strips across the plane of the most likely bite. Solves the problem. If you got a particularly tough bit of beef, cube it.

Store beef in fridge. Mix mayo about 5 parts to 2 parts A-1 and add a couple of splashes of hot sauce, to taste. Stir well and put in fridge (this is better if you do it the night before, but if you're gonna do things at the last minute, it will just have to do, won't it? Geez.). Take margarine and place about six or eight tablespoons in some tupperware. Add around three or four tablespoons of parmesan and around two crushed and minced cloves of garlic. Stir it up a lot until it's evenly mixed, return to fridge. When you're ready to make the sandwiches spread one side each of twice as many pieces of bread as you want sandwiches with the margarine/parmesan/garlic mixture. Go easy, doesn't take much and you're adding lots of salt and fat if you load it up. We're looking for flavor and color here, not a grease trap with cheese, ok? Heat up the griddle or frying pan if you don't have a griddle,
→ Clever tip #3: Most sporting goods stores sell a griddle for camp stoves made by Lodge. It's cast iron and works really well on home stoves too. It also has that ridge thing going on the other side that's pretty cool. If it's raining, snowing, hurrican-ing, tornado-ing, or you live in England, or you don't want to go outside 'cause the bugs are bad and you still want to "grill," this is just the thing.

Then you toast the bread until golden brown. My dad used to say, "when it's golden brown it's done, when it's black, down the hill you go!" We used to live at a summer resort on top of the hill, but that's another story. Set toast aside. Do some more until you are finished. Take the bread and on the not toasted side spread some of the mayo mixture.
Again, go easy, the mayo is low in saturated fat, but still has some, so discretion is the better part of valor here. Cover with beef slices, cover beef with sliced tomatoes, cover tomatoes with lettuce, spread mayo mixture on other piece of bread, again, go easy, and put it on top of the whole mess. Cut in half on the bias because I said. Garnish with either parsley or a tennis ball. You decide. Serve with beer. Newcastle brown ale is nice, or Pinstripe.

International Chinese Broccoli Beef

This dish is part of my ongoing investigation into clever uses for ground beef. When you raise your own beef or if you have me raise it for you, you get a lot of ground beef. Lots more than you can use up with sloppy joes or grilled burgers all year so here's another way to go. You're wondering why this is International. Well, seems to me meat balls are Italian, not Chinese. I'm pretty sure oatmeal is Scottish, and since Emeril uses so much garlic I'm guessing that it's Portuguese. Anyway, it tastes pretty Chinese-y. All my kids liked this dish as did my wife. This is an extremely unusual occurrence so I wrote it in the calendar.

Scurry about in a workmanlike fashion and get all this stuff together at one time:

- 2# hamburger
- Braggs Liquid Aminos—tastes like soy sauce with ¼ the sodium
- 2 # broccoli noodles
- Garlic powder
- 2 cans Swanson beef broth
- 5 flavor Chinese seasoning
- 1 # No yolk
- Srirachi hot sauce
- 1 box eggbeaters
- Onion powder
- 1 can fried noodles
- Liquid woodsmoke
- 1 cup instant oatmeal
- Cornstarch

Now, this recipe uses five flavor Chinese seasoning. Be careful with this stuff, it's seriously powerful. I once used a bit too much in a beef dish and we couldn't even get the dog to eat it. The *goats* wouldn't even eat it! So be careful. Now, make the noodles like package directions say.

Nuke or steam the broccoli until cooked but crisp, ok? Oh yeah, the broccoli should be cut into bite size chunks.

Then get a big cookie sheet and line with foil, put a baking rack on it. Put the meat in a pretty big mixing bowl, add oatmeal, egg, 1 tbls 5 flavor, ½ cup Braggs, a squirt of woodsmoke, about two tbls of onion powder, two tbls of garlic powder and maybe two squirts of Srirachi (careful, it's potent) and then just reach in there and mash all that stuff together. You can think about whatever is causing you to stress out and mash the basta. . . uh *mixture* into submission, or if you're a teen-ager, you can just stare off into the distance drooling a little. When it's all mixed shift into Italian mode and roll all the meat into 1" or so meatballs placing them on the cookie sheet. Put them into a 350 oven for 30-40 minutes.

Meanwhile, dump the 1 ½ cans broth into a small sauce pan, 'cause we're gonna make sauce, you see? And add 1 tbls 5 flavor, ½ cup Braggs, 1 tbls garlic powder, 1 tbls onion powder, two squirts of woodsmoke and bring to boil. Take the leftover half can of broth and mix well with 3 heaping tbls of cornstarch and set aside. When the meatballs are done add to broth. Return to boil. Check seasoning and add more if needed remembering always that while it has lots less sodium than soy sauce, it still has a lot, ok? Remove meatballs and set 'em aside then add the cornstarch and broth mix to saucepot and return to boil. Be careful with the heat on this, I boiled it over about three times and set off the smoke detector each time. The dog doesn't like when that goes off and barks a lot or else lays under the table and tries to cover his ears with his paws, which doesn't work all that well. The goats don't much seem to care if it goes off or not. Get a big dish and put the noodles, meatballs and broccoli in, dump the sauce evenly over the top, stir a bit. Scoop some out on a plate, garnish with fried noodles and serve with plum wine and Braggs on the side.

Lemonish Roasted Garlic Chicken Stuff

When this whole thing started, I thought, geez, I'm never gonna be able to cook low fat, low salt or low anything else for that matter. I mean really, I'm over six foot tall! Low just doesn't compute. But a man's gotta do what a man's gotta do, so I did this--I got all this stuff together on a backpacking trip from the post office to the Grocery Store:

4 chicken breasts, skinless, all
   visible fat removed
1 can low salt fat free chicken broth
½ cup flour
3 tbls olive oil
¼ cup lemon juice
1 tbl Tarragon
2 tbls Garlic powder
2 tbls Onion powder
2 tbls Roasted garlic
1tsp Cayenne pepper
1tsp Seasoned pepper
Rice, no yolk noodles, bowties, those
   flower shaped noodles or oh, well,
     just any noodles I guess.

Once I finally got home from my ultra-healthy hike, I took and browned chicken breasts in non-stick pan with about 1 tbls of olive oil on medium heat. When they started to stick, I slopped a bit of the chicken stock in there. When cooked through, I took 'em all out and deglazed the pan with chicken broth. Then I added flour, 2 tbls oil, the rest of the chicken stock and all the seasonings. I brought it to a boil, and adjusted thickness—you want it about the same consistency as 90 weight gear oil—more flour if too thin, a bit of water if too thick. Then I reduced the heat and simmered for 13-21 minutes. I checked seasonings, reseasoned if necessary, simmered a bit longer, returned the chicken to the pan, heated and served it over some rice. But it's gonna be good over pasta, rice or mashed potatoes or maybe potato chips, but wait! Those aren't on the diet so don't use 'em. Oh! You can have a glass of good white wine with 'em too, 'cause they've found out a glass of wine a day actually helps your heart. Hah!!

Get Stuffed with Mexican Stuffing

You can use this stuff to stuff stuff. Like tortillas or taco shells or cabbage rolls or bell peppers or puff pastry or your face. You could stuff your mailbox with it, but that will likely attract stray dogs, cats and skunks so I disrecommend it. Besides the mail carrier will probably get upset and you don't' want to annoy those folks! As always, the ingredients are not etched in stone, so 'speriment as you will.

2 pounds ground beef
1 can no salt kidney beans
1 can no salt chili beans
2 cups niblitized corn
Masa flour
chopped roasted garlic
Cumin
Coriander
Cilantro
chipotle powder
Liquid smoke
Chicken broth

Take the beef and make 4 relatively huge hamburger patties. No, we're not making hamburgers and get off my back, just follow the directions, willya? Heat up the barbie, when hot reduce temp to medium low and slap the patties on there. Cook until well done turning once. What you have accomplished is to remove most of the fat in the hamburger meat, you clever person you. Let 'em cool a bit then haul 'em back into the kitchen where you'll bust 'em up in a big skillet. Dust with about ¼ cup of masa flour, add all the spices to taste but about 3 tbls garlic, 2 tbls cumin, 1 tbl coriander, 2 tbls cilantro, 1 tbl chipotle and about ¼ to ½ cup of chicken broth. Cook a while then add drained beans and corn and smoke. Add more broth to a thick stew like consistency. If you get it too thin add more flour. Cook for a while. Take mixture and stuff something. Would be good with margaritas, w'thout salt of course.

Nuna Turtle Casserole Lofatsalt

Ok, well you've had some tuna helper at one time or another and some of it is pretty good. Some of it sucks. But imagine your family or guests surprise and delight when you tell 'em you made *this* tuna casserole *from scratch!* Ok well maybe they won't wet themselves with joy, but it does taste a lot better than the mixes. Oh, yeah, the name. Seems my spouse was having a bit of a dyslexic moment when she tried to say, "Gee, this is the best Tuna Noodle Casserole I've ever had." While she sometimes can't speak, she has excellent taste in Nuna Turtle Casseroles.

Get all this stuff, and get it all at the same time:

- Two cans tuna, drained, or use those foil pouch thingies, try the hickory smoke flavored
- One package pasta, I prefer shells but get what the voices tell you to
- 1 cup, more or less of frozen peas
- Olive oil
- ½ cup or so of white flour
- One slice purple onion
- Juice of one lemon
- 4 cans condensed skim milk
- Pepper, fresh from a mill is more better
- Cilantro
- Liquid woodsmoke
- Grated cheddar cheese
- Grated parmesan cheese
- Hot Hungarian paprika

Do all this, in this order:

Get a pot that'll be big enough for the pasta, remember I like shells and for all you anal-retentive folks out there, you won't be following the recipe if you use anything else. Put the water in the pot and add a couple good cranks of the mill of pepper , a couple drops of the liquid smoke, and about a teaspoon of cilantro. When the water comes to a boil add the pasta and cook per package directions. You might want to leave it a bit al dente (not quite done for you non-Italian speakers) as it will cook a bit in the casserole. Drain and hold. No, that doesn't mean stand there with the pot in your hand, just set it aside someplace, willya? Geez . . .

While the pasta's cookin' put about 2 tbls olive oil and ¼ cup chicken broth in a medium sauce pan. Saute the onion slice you already chopped up for four or five minutes. Add the flour. Make a white roux (cook the flour a bit in the oil and broth over medium low heat). When done add to the roux with some milk. Ok, now listen closely. Just add a little milk, say half a can, and mix it in. You want it to end up the consistency of about 40-weight motor oil. You're not gonna use the whole four cans, but that's what we keep in the pantry at our house and the amount of milk you add depends on how much flour you added and the phases of the moon and how the Broncos are doing this year and like that, so it's best to have the whole four cans out. Ok? Besides, you'll need that on the shelf for other stuff anyway. Add pepper to taste, 1 tbl cilantro, the lemon juice a good squirt of woodsmoke and 1 tsp paprika.   When it's cooked a while, add the peas and the tuna, cook on low for not very long.

Meanwhile, get a medium casserole dish, one of the rectangular ones, and grease it with. Now take the roux mixture and mix it with the pasta the shovel it into the dish. Sprinkle the top with cheddar, then parmesan and bake for 40 minutes at 350 degrees Fahrenheit.

Pull it out of the oven when it beeps or whatever and serve with a spatula, garnish with paprika and a sprig of whatever green you have laying about—you could use orchard grass 'cause everything eats that stuff anyway.

Spanish Rice

Normally I'd have some clever repartee' at this point, but I'm just not in the mood today. You'll just have to talk amongst yourselves for amusement and leave me out of it. Just make the rice and some tacos and beans and leave me alone. Think I'll go ride my motorcycle. Bye.

Get all this:

2 cups rice
1 14 oz. Can diced tomatoes, no salt
2 14 oz. Cans of water
Cilantro
Cumin
Coriander
Cholula hot sauce
Liquid Smoke

Put tomatoes and water and 1tbl each cilantro, coriander, 2 tbl cumin, several good squirts of Cholula and about ½ tsp of liquid smoke into a sauce pan, heat to boiling, add rice, reduce to low heat and cover for 15 minutes, check tenderness of rice, reseason and serve with other Mexican-ish stuff.

Ok. I'm back, but now I'm tired instead of grumpy. I had my youngest make the rice, we've got some leftover chicken and the little woman opened some wine. So I'm for all that and as for the rest of you, well, carry on my wayward, uh, cooks?

Southwestern Pork and Beans

I was thinking one day, "You know, there are these beans, I've seen them in the store, what are they called? Northern? No, *Great* Northern beans. That's it! I ought to make something out of beans with such a cool name as that!" And I did. Naturally, with a name like *Great* Northern Beans, you just have to call it Southwestern. So I did.

Stuff:
1 2# pork loin
2 cans no salt Chick Peas (Garbanzos)
3 cans no salt Great Northern white beans
2 12 0z jars Herdez mild green salsa
2 cups rice

Slap pork loin on the barbecue for 12 minutes a side, remove to kitchen, rest for 20 minutes (the pork, not you), then cube pork loin, about 1/2". Open and drain chick peas, dump into stock pot. Open great northerns and dump into stock pot, dump in salsas. Dump in pork. Simmer for a long time. Cook rice. Put rice in bowls, put pork and beans on top of rice. Eat.

Note: If you were looking at this recipe in order to generate gas for some special event, be aware--chick peas and white beans don't generate all that much gas. If you wan to enhance your flatulence, eat pinto beans, especially refried frijoles pintos. And if you really want to be spectacular, have some frijoles refritos while taking Zocor and eating coleslaw. Nuclear!

Tuna Tacos a Little Wong

This time of year my fancy turns to stuff that's not all that hot, temperature wise, since that's all taken care of by the weather. So I try to make stuff that's pretty tasty but not real heat-hot, even if it's got a bit of hot sauce bite. Now you have to understand, my kids love tuna. They like it in tuna salad, sandwiches, out of the can and out of the pouch. They even love tekka maki, or for the uninitiated, raw tuna roll sushi. So I figured I'd give them a gourmet treat and I made this truly wonderful seared yellowfin tuna steak. You know the kind, seared on the outside and raw on the inside, yum! I don't know why, but I was shocked when they whined they didn't like it! I had to nuke the little darlings (the tuna steaks, not the kids) before they'd eat it. So what can you say, kids are kids. Well it gave me this idea for tuna tacos that goes something like this:

Get all this stuff:
1# tuna, yellowfin, ahi, whatever they've got
Taco shells
Taco/nacho cheese
Angelhair coleslaw
Mayonnaise
Non fat yogurt
Non fat sour cream
Cholula hot sauce Pace salsa picante, medium
Soy sauce—actually, use Braggs Liquid Aminos instead, less than ¼ the sodium and all the taste
Unseasoned rice vinegar

Cholula hot sauce
Cumin
Coriander
Cilantro
Dried ginger
Allspice
Ketchup
Juice of 2 lemons
Baking soda
Fresh melon salad from the store.

Look at that list again, see anything a bit, um, *wong, uh, I mean wrong?* How 'bout the soy sauce? Dried ginger? Wait for it, it'll all come clear.

Now do all this:
Get a mixing bowl and dump about 1 cup mayo, 1 cup sour cream, 1 cup yogurt, 2 tbls each of cumin, coriander and cilantro, a pinch of baking soda, 1 cup salsa, the lemon juice, a good squirt of Cholula and ½ cup of ketchup. Mix it all together with a whisk and stick it in the icebox. When it's been in there at least 15 minutes--half an hour would be better--taste, adjust seasoning, and put enough on the coleslaw to cover without making it all yucky and soggy, use less than you think you need, 'cause while you can always add more, taking it out is a pain. Put it in the icebox.

While that's chillin', take your tuna and put in a baggie that contains 1 cup rice wine vinegar, ½ cup Braggs, 2 tbls dried ginger, ¼ tsp allspice and a good squirt of Cholula. Marinate in fridge for ½ hour at least. Take tuna and stick it on the gas grill. What? You have a charcoal grill? Well use that then. Jeez, I do give you some credit for independent thought. Anyway, the grill should be hot and you don't want to cook the tuna too long, 2 or 3 minutes a side then whisk it away to the kitchen where you'll dump it in a mixing bowl and shred with a fork. Whew!

Now take your taco shells and stuff 'em with tuna meat, sprinkle a bit of cheese on the meat. Snag the coleslaw out of the icebox, slap a healthy dollop on each taco, and serve with the fruit salad as a starter. You'll see, the soy sauce, rice vinegar, ginger and allspice makes it all pretty *wong,* and pretty good too! Now, crack open a Pacifico and get to it!

Desserts

Emergency Preparedness for Dessert Disaster

Now most nights there are cookies in the jar, or sherbet in the freezer or pie on the counter. Sometimes you have to settle for the semi-yucky cookies the kids picked out, or a piece of apple pie that's been around long enough it's starting to turn to apple flavored rubber, but it's still dessert. Then there are those times when through some administrative oversight, or screw-uppery in the upper echelons and you finish dinner to find *there is no dessert!* OHMIGOD! What now? After we get done blaming George Bush, I mean. Well, gentle reader, I'm here to tell you, it's not as bad as you thought, there's always a dessert hiding in the house somewhere, so have faith and read on!

Emergency preparedness! If you're going to survive a dessert disaster, you're need a few things on hand so go get all this stuff:

- Frozen tortillas
- Frozen loaf of your favorite bread
- Rice, frozen if leftover, or dry
- Crackers, low sodium
- Milk, if you're perpetually out, it *will* freeze
- Margarine
- Canned pie filling
- Honey
- Ground cinnamon, mixed with granulated sugar
- Frozen puff pastry
- Smart Balance

Antique recipes from Texas and Missouri--My dad was from Texas, my mom from Southern Missouri. They had some clever if odd makeshift desserts, so here they are:
- Bill's milk and crackers—take a large glass, crush crackers into it, add milk to the top, bang it on the counter once to get the air bubbles out, top off with milk and eat with a spoon.
- Thelma's milque toast—same glass, same milk, but substitute torn up pieces of toast and add sugar. Or just plain bread will work. Sourdough is particularly interesting. Also surprisingly good.
- Bill's poorman's rice puddin'—put the rice in a glass, top with a couple tablespoons of sugar, pour in the milk and eat with a spoon. This is particularly yummy if the rice is still warm. Jake's favorite, too.

Fakin' it with puff pastry
- Get out the puff pastry, thaw, get a can of pie filling, stick a dollop onto the pastry, fold over and bake per instructions. Poof! Instant turnovers. In a pinch, use jam or jelly for filling.
- Spread thawed puff pastry with margarine dump a sizeable pile of sugar and cinnamon on top, fold over and bake. Or use honey and cinnamon.

Desert a la Mexico!
- Take some flour tortillas, spread with margarine, dump a bunch of cinnamon sugar on top, roll up like a tacquito and nuke for 15 seconds or so. Fold it in the middle so it doesn't all leak out the end.
- Same as above with pie filling, jelly or jam. Apple butter is particularly good and for any of these if you put the barest sprinkle of cayenne pepper on it, you'll give it an interesting bite.
- Gringo sopapillas--Take tortilla chips, heat in the microwave and drizzle honey over them, serve with wet and dry paper towels.
- Genuine imitation sopapillas—take puff pastry triangles and bake, sprinkle with powdered sugar and serve with honey and wet and dry paper towels.

Your ideas--Think something up! C'mon, get up right now and go look in the pantry, surely there's something in there you can cobble together. Grab that chocolate bar you've been hiding under your bed and sandwich a chunk in crackers, nuke for 5 seconds and serve. Got marshmallows? Same thing with them and instant fake s'mores. Or, get bizarre--celery with jelly or jam, nuked carrots with margarine, sugar and cinnamon. Remember, if it doesn't work and your creation is yucky, it'll go in the compost bin, and you're no worse off than you were before you did it. Besides you can still go down to the Mini-merc and get some hot tamales candy, which amazingly actually fits into a heart healthy diet. Go figure.

The Great Fruit Massacre!

No, no, Igor! It's *macerate* not massacre! Can't you get anything right? I really have to start typing my own recipes. Hungarian hunchback assistants just aren't what they used to be. I didn't want to kill any fruit, I wanted to soak some stuff in other stuff so it gets all juicy and sweet and stuff. So we will, 'cause bein's it's pretty hot and bein's it's summer and all, or at least is was when I wrote this, seemed to me I should do something clever with cool stuff for desert. So I did.

Sally forth and gather at least two items, all fresh, from the following list:
Strawberries
Blueberries
Raspberries
Blackberries
Peaches
Nectarines
Plums
Whatever other fresh fruit cranks your tractor

And get all of these:
Applesauce
1 each raspberry, pineapple, lime and rainbow sherbet
Sugar

Now do all this:
Take the fruit and if it's big, like strawberries or plums, halve or quarter it. If it's fuzzy like peaches, peel it first. Dump it in a big bowl. If you're using black, blue or raspberries, then take about a quarter of 'em and mash 'em. Sprinkle on about a ½ cup of sugar, powdered is nice but not necessary. Stir. Refrigerate. Wait. Overnight would be best, but at least half an hour. This is called "macerating." Cool word, no?
You can add red wine or a little vodka or rum, maybe even some balsamic vinegar. I haven't tried it but I'm guessing that even 7-up would work. Experiment and if you come up with something killer, write in and tell me about it.
Now comes the option part.

Option 1: put about a cup of apple sauce in a wine glass, top with macerated fruit and garnish with a sprig of mint.

Option 2: Take about two cups of fruit mixture puree in a blender, fill a wine glass halfway with fruit, put a layer of puree and top with fruit. Sprig with mint again. You could also add a dollop of sherbet to the puree, try different flavors.

Option 3: put a large spoonful of fruit in a bowl. Top with sherbet of your choice, plop a cherry on top of that.

Option 4: soften all four sherbets in the microwave then get a tall water glass, and layer fruit and all the different sherbets.

Option 5: just eat the sherbet one night, and the chilled fruit the next. Simplify!

Option 6: you figure something out, the write me and tell me about it.

Conclusion

What this book is really about is freedom. There's lots of talk about it, but the bottom line is this. Live in the USA. Have all the rights and privileges. But if you can't walk around, if you can't breathe, if you can't do what you want to do, you aren't free. It's my hope that if we can all start cooking leaner, getting a little exercise, the maybe we can take advantage of the freedoms our country provides. Oh, and incidentally if by gaining some freedom by using this book you give *me* a little financial freedom by telling all your friends to buy the book, that would be good too.

Thanks,
Fat Jack

About the Author

Fat Jack is actually John P. White, born in Las Vegas, Nevada about midway through the 20th century, and raised in Mammoth Lakes, California in the summers and Los Angeles in the winters. Mammoth was better. He attended California Lutheran College for many years with few results other than finding his one true love and soulmate, Beth. They moved back to Las Vegas in 1976 for 25 years of semi-crappy jobs and raising kids. He returned to college at UNLV and received a Bachelor's, cum Laude in History in 1996. In 2000 they moved to beautiful Bayfield, Colorado and continue to live there to this very day. John has been, variously, a ski equipment, shoe, vacuum cleaner, used car, sporting goods, motorcycle and other things salesman. He has been a certified ski technician and boot fitter, journeyman drywall hanger, armored car guard, driver and truck commander, substitute, high and middle school teacher, muzzleloading gun store owner, parking lot sweeping company owner, short order cook, busboy, dishwasher, maid, garbage man, housewife, and probably a few other things we've left out. He has released one CD, "Out Standing in His Field" of self-written blues and rock music and he hopes to eventually sell a few copies. A re-release of most of the songs on his first CD and some new ones called "Blender Blues" will soon be available as will his next CD "Bad Afro." He is at present an unsuccessful farmer/rancher and landlord. For slow news weeks, he writes a column in the Pine River Times weekly newspaper called "Fat Jack Cooks Stuff."

Thanks

To Janet Wilson at Mercy Medical for talking me into writing this, as well as all the nurses down there—Cathy, Carmen, Susan and all the rest. Melanie Brubaker-Mazur for publishing my drivel in the paper. Beth for not throwing me out long ago. My kids, Jake, Mickey, Shannon and The German Kid Eiko for providing a pool of test subjects for my recipes.

Legaleze

All the stuff you got with this book is copyrighted, © 2007 John P. White, all rights are reserved and no part of this book may be used, copied or whatnot without prior written permission from me, that would be John P. White, so there.

Contact

You can contact me at:
John P. White
P.O. box 286
Bayfield, CO 81122
Email: freepowder@wildblue.net

Music

In my spare time I cut this really, really good CD cleverly entitled, "J.P. White, Out Standing in His Field," and you can get it at WWW.CDBABY.COM/jpwhite or by searching on "J. P. White" on I-tunes. Look for new albums, "Blender Blues" and "Bad Afro" soon.

**Now, go and sin no more, uh no, wait, um,
Now, go and cook some more!**
Yeah, that's it.
Oh, and have fun.

www.ingramcontent.com/pod-product-compliance
Ingram Content Group UK Ltd.
Pitfield, Milton Keynes, MK11 3LW, UK
UKHW051303180426
11947UKWH00020B/1875